A CourseGuide for

Introduction to Biblical Interpretation

**William W. Klein
Craig L. Blomberg
Robert L. Hubbard, Jr.**

ZONDERVAN
ACADEMIC

ZONDERVAN ACADEMIC

A CourseGuide for Introduction to Biblical Interpretation

Copyright © 2019 by Zondervan

ISBN 978-0-310-11066-8 (softcover)

Requests for information should be addressed to:
Zondervan, *3900 Sparks Dr. SE, Grand Rapids, Michigan 49546*

CONTENTS

Introduction

Welcome to *A CourseGuide for Introduction to Biblical Interpretation*. These guides were created for formal and informal students alike who want to engage deeper in biblical, theological, or ministry studies. We hope this guide will provide an opportunity for you to grow not only in your understanding, but also in your faith.

How to Use this Guide

This guide is meant to be used in conjunction with the book *Introduction to Biblical Interpretation* and its corresponding videos, *Introduction to Biblical Interpretation Video Lectures*. After you have read each chapter in the book and watched the accompanying video lesson, the materials in this guide will help you review and assess what you have learned. Application-oriented questions are included as well. For additional practice, you will want to complete exercises found in *Introduction to Biblical Interpretation Workbook*.

Each CourseGuide has been individually designed to best equip you in your studies, but in general, you can expect the following components. Most CourseGuides begin every chapter with a "You Should Know" section, which highlights key terminology, people, and facts to remember. This section serves as a helpful summary for directing your studies. Reflection questions, typically two to three per chapter, prompt you to summarize key points you've learned. Discussion questions invite you to an even deeper level of engagement. Finally, most chapters will end with a short quiz to test your retention. You can find the answer key to each quiz at the bottom of the page following it.

For Further Study

CourseGuides accompany books and videos from some of the world's top biblical and theological scholars. They may be used independently, or in small groups or classrooms, offering quality instruction to equip students for academic and ministry pursuits. If you would like to engage in further study with Zondervan's CourseGuides, the full lineup may be viewed online. After completing your studies with *A CourseGuide for Introduction to Biblical Interpretation*, we recommend moving on to *A CourseGuide for How to Read the Bible for All Its Worth* and *A CourseGuide for Know How We Got Our Bible*.

CHAPTER 1

The Need for Interpretation

You Should Know

- Hermeneutics describes the task of explaining the meaning of the Scriptures.

- How illumination of the Holy Spirit helps believers understand Scripture: convinces readers the Bible is true; gives readers the ability to apprehend the meaning; and gives conviction that leads readers to embrace its meaning

- Locution: the particular words or sentences that are written or spoken in a statement or discourse

- Illocution: the intention of the speaker or writer in using particular words

- Perlocution: what the speaker or author envisioned the outcome of his or her words to be on the listener or reader

- Types of word meanings: referential — what a word refers to; denotative — direct meaning of the world; connotative — suggestive sense that grows out of the denotative meaning; and contextual — specific sense suggested by a word's use in context

- Four distances that hermeneutics must overcome: distance of time; distance of culture; distance of geography; and distance of language

- Exegesis: drawing the meaning out of a text, from the Greek word *exēgeomai*, meaning "to explain"

- Univocal: the use of terms restricted to one meaning; such statements have the same meaning for the original writer or readers as they do for us

- Analogical: the use of terms with a proportional meaning, partly the same and partly different for original and modern readers

Reflection Questions

1. Some say the only correct meaning of a text is the meaning intended by the original author. Others say discovering meaning is more of a function of the reader. What do you think? Why?

2. It is important for Bible readers to distinguish between the idea that the Bible was written "for me" from the idea it was written "to me." What are the differences? Have you considered this distinction before? How does it affect the way you approach the Bible?

3. How do you balance the assertion that "We cannot simply pick up the Bible and read it like a familiar book" with the historic faith practice of devotional reading of Scripture? Is devotional reading misguided? What is its role?

Discussion Question

1. Have you consciously thought about the task of hermeneutics in the past, or have you been more inclined to simply read the Bible and "believe what it says"? How does thinking about hermeneutics impact how you read the Bible? What does reading the Bible "correctly" mean to you? How do we do it?

Quiz

1. Hermeneutics means:
    a) The study of the social relations in the New Testament
    b) The task of explaining the meaning of the Scriptures
    c) The discipline of preaching God's Word
    d) The study of the Holy Spirit

2. (T/F) The idea that the Holy Spirit simply and clearly tells people what the Bible means is simplistic and potentially dangerous.

3. (T/F) The role of the Holy Spirit in understanding God's Word is indispensable.

4. (T/F) Interpretation is a science, not an art.

5. (T/F) Responsible hermeneutics must give attention to both the original context of the text and to the circumstances and understandings of those who seek to interpret it.

6. (T/F) It is possible to interpret without any preunderstanding of the subject.

7. (T/F) The biblical writers primarily developed original literary forms and conventions, which are not reflected in the broader ancient culture.

8. (T/F) Christian Bible readers should avoid approaching the Bible with the tools of literary criticism.

9. (T/F) We cannot derive the meaning of a text without first examining its form.

10. Theological Interpretation of Scripture (TIS):
    a) Means readers only study Scripture after mastering systematic theology
    b) Studies Scripture only for what it teaches about the doctrine of God, ignoring the rest
    c) Maintains the theological nature of Scripture and embraces the influence of theology upon the reader
    d) Insists that interpreters stand "over" Scripture, since they have two thousand years of church history from which to draw

CHAPTER 2

The History of Interpretation

You Should Know

- The Septuagint (LXX) is a Greek translation of the Hebrew Bible, beginning in 285 BC; later became the Bible of the early church

- Midrash aims to uncover the deeper meanings that the rabbis assumed were inherent in the actual wording of Scripture.

- How the Apostles interpreted the Old Testament: literal interpretation; literal-contextual interpretation; and principle/application interpretation

- Typology refers to identifying events, objects, ideas, and other divinely inspired patterns or symbols represented in the Old Testament that anticipate God's activity later in history.

- Augustine's first principle of interpretation specifies that it aims to lead readers to love God and other people

- Jerome's translation from Hebrew and Greek manuscripts, known as the Vulgate (from the Latin word for "common"), became the official Bible of the Western church.

- The four meanings of Scripture according to many medieval scholars: literal—what actually happened; allegorical—what to believe; moral—what to do; and anagogical— what to hope for

- Source criticism: a discipline arising in the nineteenth century in which scholars seek to discover the sources behind a text

- Redaction criticism: seeks to discern the distinctive theological and thematic emphases that the individual biblical writers or editors gave their materials

Reflection Questions

1. Do you think allegorical interpretation is a valid approach to hermeneutics? Why or why not? Luther rejected the allegorical method of interpretation but promoted the typological method of interpretation. Explain the differences.

2. Do you think Luther's conviction of Scripture as the sole authority, as opposed to Scripture plus the church, opens the door for people to interpret Scripture any way they like? Why or why not? How can this danger be avoided?

3. The Anabaptists and Mennonites applied the Reformation principles of *sola scriptura* and the perspicuity of Scripture in ways the Reformers strongly opposed. What do you appreciate about the emphases of the pietist movement? Where do you see the continuing influence of this movement? What are some possible dangers, based on what you read about pietism?

Discussion Question

1. Name several of the varying interpretive approaches to Scripture outlined in this session. What do you make of this diversity of interpretive approaches to Scripture in the twenty-first century? Which ones stuck out to you? What are the strengths or dangers about so many current approaches to Scripture?

Quiz

1. The Septuagint is the _____ translation of the Hebrew Scriptures, dating from around 285 BC.

    a) Aramaic
    b) Greek

    c) Latin

    d) Syriac

2. The Qumran community was most preoccupied with the _____ of the Hebrew Bible.

    a) Law of Moses

    b) Wisdom literature

    c) Prophets

    d) Record of kings

3. Early Christian interpreters revered Jesus as the new:

    a) Moses

    b) Samuel

    c) Elijah

    d) Isaiah

4. The most popular interpretive approach among the fathers (AD 100–150) was:

    a) Literal-contextual

    b) Reader-response

    c) Anagogical

    d) Allegorical

5. (T/F) Typographical interpretation of Scripture was generally rejected by early Christian interpreters.

6. (T/F) Origen taught that the wise interpreter of Scripture should focus only on its literal, straightforward sense.

7. (T/F) Emperor Constantine played a significant role in pressuring the church to settle its differences and to standardize its disputed doctrines.

8. (T/F) Early Christian interpreters approached Scripture in an altogether different way than their Jewish contemporaries.

9. More than any of his contemporaries, Thomas Aquinas emphasized the _____ interpretation of Scripture.

    a) Allegorical

    b) Anagogical

c) Moral
d) Literal

10. The two towering figures of post-World War I interpretation are
   a) Moltmann and Pannenberg
   b) Kierkegaard and Heidegger
   c) Barth and Bultmann
   d) Schweitzer and Jeremias

CHAPTER 3

Literary and Social-Scientific Approaches to Interpretation

You Should Know

- Literary criticism is largely ahistorical in nature, interested in examining only the final form of the text.

- Narrative criticism focuses on plot, theme, motifs, characterization, style, figures of speech, symbolism, foreshadowing, repetition, speed of time in narrative, point of view, etc.

- Common convictions and values of postmodernism: ideological pluralism; impossibility of objectivity in interpretation; importance of community in shaping perspective; rejection of negative modernist evaluation of spirituality; formative role of narrative in understanding our lives; and language as determinative of thought and meaning

- Critical realism is an approach that involves the dialogical process between interpreter and texts in which one successfully approximates true meaning, even if never comprehensively capturing it.

- Reader-response criticism claims that meaning is the product of individual readers in interaction with the texts; there is no objective meaning in the text itself.

- Deconstruction seeks to show how all texts undermine themselves and therefore make no absolute claims on readers.

- Ideologically, deconstruction derives from the nineteenth-century nihilist philosopher Friedrich Nietzsche and his recent disciple, Jacques Derrida.

- Liberation theology initially developed as an engaged Roman Catholic response in Latin America to centuries of oppression against the mostly indigenous poor residents by ruling elites in society, government, and church.

- Postcolonialism is a branch of cultural criticism which seeks to ensure that the yearnings of the poor take precedence over the interests of the affluent, and often accepts religious pluralism.

- Queer theology: seeks to embrace all sexual minorities under one label, examining the interpretive possibilities of "queer" when applied to any unusual feature of human behavior in Scripture

Reflection Questions

1. Does the fact that evangelicals believe the *final form* of the text is inspired and authoritative undermine any reasons to use historical-critical tools for interpretation? In what ways might historical-critical tools still benefit evangelical readers?

2. How do you respond to the view that meaning is the product of the individual reader? Where have you seen people treat the Bible this way?

3. How do liberation interpreters make their case from the Bible? What texts are most important? What do you make of their position and claims, from a hermeneutical standpoint? What possible problems with this hermeneutic did you read?

Discussion Question

1. How do you handle the tension of showing God's unconditional love to others while at the same time not approving what you believe contradicts God's will? Where have you faced this tension in your own experience? What did you do?

Quiz

1. Narrative critics often assume when they study the Bible as literature that the texts must be viewed as:
    a) Fiction
    b) History
    c) Proclamation
    d) Redemptive

2. Liberation theology initially developed as an engaged _____ response in Latin America to centuries of oppression of mostly indigenous poor residents by the ruling elites.
    a) Baptist
    b) Roman Catholic
    c) Pentecostal
    d) Reformed

3. Liberation theologians hold that God has a preferential option for the:
    a) Well-educated
    b) Hard-working
    c) Poor
    d) Aged

4. The liberationist writer, José Miranda, equated Christianity with:
    a) Communism
    b) Capitalism
    c) Colonialism
    d) Ancient Israel

5. (T/F) In liberation theology, theory takes precedence over experience.

6. (T/F) Literary criticism is ahistorical in nature and interested only in examining the final form of the text.

7. (T/F) There are black and African characters in Scripture who are not necessarily so recognized by white readers.

8. (T/F) Evangelical or biblical feminists do not believe that the Bible promotes full equality of the sexes.

9. (T/F) All five of the women appearing in Matthew's genealogy of Jesus found themselves in morally ambiguous situations.

10. (T/F) Careful interpreters of Scripture ought to reject out of hand any interpretive ideas of various advocacy groups that seem new or possibly scandalous.

CHAPTER 4

The Canon and Translation

You Should Know

- The canon of Scripture refers to the collection of books that Christians accept as uniquely authoritative.

- Roman Catholic and Eastern Orthodox Bibles preserve various apocryphal or deutero-canonical books that are not found in Protestant Bibles.

- Marcion was a second-century heretic who believed that Jesus and the God of the Old Testament were opposites. He developed a "canon" of an edited Gospel of Luke and some Pauline Epistles, but nothing else.

- The Muratorian Fragment is probably the earliest manuscript containing a list of New Testament books to be viewed as Scripture, dating from the late second century AD.

- Origen was the first Christian writer to refer to all twenty-seven books in our New Testament, in the early third century AD, but notes that six were disputed.

- Three criteria for New Testament canonicity: apostolicity; orthodoxy; and catholicity

- The autographs of Scripture are the original documents penned by the original biblical writers, to which we no longer have access.

- Formally equivalent translations prioritize accurately preserving the form and structure of the original text over what is the most intelligible English.

- Dynamically equivalent translations prioritize clarity over grammar and syntax while still being true to the meaning of the text.

- 1611: the year in which the translation of the King James Version of the English Bible (the "authorized" version) was completed

Reflection Questions

1. How do you respond to the centuries-long process of the canon of Scripture becoming firm? What do you make of the human element of identifying and affirming what books do and do not constitute Scripture? How might some find this challenging?

2. Why do you think God would allow variants in the biblical manuscripts, even if they are minor? How do you reconcile the doctrines of inerrancy and inspiration with the fact scholars sometimes need to resort to their best guess in order to identify what was most likely the original wording of text?

3. Do you prefer an English translation that prioritizes the original form and structure of the text but is more wooden, or do you prefer an English translation that captures the meaning in better-sounding English but does not rigorously follow the form of the original text? Why?

Discussion Question

1. How would you respond to someone who believes the King James Version of the English Bible is the only inspired Bible and should be the only translation English readers use? Why do you think there are those who so stridently argue this opinion?

Quiz

1. At Qumran copies of all the undisputed Old Testament books have been found except for:
   a) Song of Songs
   b) Esther

   c) Ruth

   d) Jonah

2. Most English Bibles order the books of the Old Testament according to their arrangement in the:

   a) Hebrew Bible

   b) Septuagint

   c) Vulgate

   d) Mishnah

3. Matthew was placed first among the Gospels in the New Testament canon because:

   a) It was written first

   b) It was understood as most important

   c) It provides the clearest link with the Old Testament

   d) Early Christians cast lots to determine the order

4. (T/F) It is reasonable to conclude that Jews agreed upon the boundaries of the Hebrew canon in New Testament times.

5. (T/F) Protestants, Catholics, and Orthodox Christians have never agreed on the extent of the Old Testament.

6. (T/F) Jews at the time of Jesus accepted the so-called apocryphal or deutero-canonical books as authoritative Scripture.

7. (T/F) Pauline authorship of Hebrews was not doubted until the rise of modern textual criticism in the nineteenth century.

8. (T/F) There has been less agreement among Christians as to what books comprise the New Testament than about what books comprise the Old Testament.

9. (T/F) Two of the later New Testament books refer to earlier Christian writings as Scripture.

10. (T/F) Six of the books in our New Testament were disputed in the early centuries AD due to internal evidence (i.e., issues arising from the material found within the book itself).

ANSWER KEY

1. B, 2. B, 3. C, 4. T, 5. T, 6. F, 7. F, 8. F, 9. T, 10. T

CHAPTER 5

The Interpreter

You Should Know

- Qualifications of the interpreter of Scripture: a reasoned faith in the God who reveals; willingness to obey its message; willingness to apply appropriate methods; illumination of the Holy Spirit; and membership in the church

- Evangelical presuppositions about the nature of the Bible: a divine/human book; authoritative and true; a spiritual document; unified and diverse; understandable; and forming a canon as Holy Scripture

- Inerrancy implies that what God authored in the Bible contains no errors.

- Infallibility refers to Scripture's Spirit-driven ability to achieve God's purposes.

- Neo-orthodox theologians argue that the Bible only becomes the word of God as believers faithfully read, preach, and apprehend its message.

- *Regula fidei*:"the rule of faith"; the principle of interpreting the Bible according to orthodox Christian understanding

- The goal of hermeneutics is to enable interpreters to arrive at the meaning of the text that the biblical writers or editors intended their readers to understand.

- How to engage the fact of presuppositions: admit that you have presuppositions; identify those presuppositions that you bring to the task; evaluate your presuppositions; embrace those presuppositions you believe are valid; and take steps to jettison those presuppositions you deem invalid.

- Presuppositionalists begin the interpretive process by assuming such tenets as God's existence or the truthfulness of revelation in the Bible.

Reflection Questions

1. How can the reader know whether his or her interpretation has been aided by the work of the Holy Spirit? Where have you observed people relying on the Holy Spirit at the expense of using appropriate interpretive methods and techniques? What were the results?

2. Why do you think God allowed so much diversity within the canon of Scripture? Why not instead recount exactly what happened, only once? What might be the benefits for readers?

3. You read that preunderstandings can be viewed either as a desirable asset or as a treacherous culprit. In what ways can they be an asset? In what ways a culprit? How would you characterize your own preunderstandings?

Discussion Question

1. Explain the analogy of the two chemists. Do you agree that the Bible interpreter with more education and experience will come to the most valid interpretations? Why or why not? Where does this leave those Bible readers who do not have training in hermeneutics?

Quiz

1. The essential qualification for a full understanding of the Bible is:
    a) Strong knowledge of ancient Hebrew and Greek
    b) Skills in literary analysis of the text of the Bible
    c) To know God and believe he is speaking through the Bible
    d) Careful attention to the syntax and grammar

2. For the Christian, _____ is an indispensable ingredient for the proper understanding of Scripture.

    a) Prayer
    b) *Lectio divina*
    c) Historical knowledge
    d) Bible memorization

3. Throughout much of church history, Christians assumed the unity of Scripture and downplayed its:

    a) Contradictions
    b) Diversity
    c) Polytheism
    d) Errors

4. (T/F) The process of canonization granted authority to the books of Scripture.

5. (T/F) Good interpreters bring no preunderstandings with them when they examine a text.

6. (T/F) There has been a recent shift in the practice of biblical interpretation which favors reader-centered approaches instead of author- or text-centered approaches.

7. (T/F) A historical focus provides the best avenue to a legitimate literary reading of Scripture.

8. (T/F) Interpreters should test their preunderstandings to see whether they correspond to the biblical data.

9. (T/F) Because of one's epistemological restrictions, the Christian position at bottom level is ultimately a "leap in the dark."

10. (T/F) There is an informed circularity to one's commitment to the authority of Scripture based on one's prior commitment to its truthfulness and its status as divine revelation.

ANSWER KEY
1. C, 2. A, 3. B, 4. F, 5. F, 6. T, 7. T, 8. T, 9. F, 10. T

CHAPTER 6

The Goal of Interpretation

You Should Know

- Potential meanings in a text: the meaning the author intends to convey; the meaning a reader understands; and the actual meaning conveyed by the words and grammar of the text

- *Sensus Plenior:* Latin for "fuller sense"; the idea that the Holy Spirit may have encoded meaning into a text beyond what was intended by the human author

- The Teacher of Righteousness was the founder and early leader of the Qumran community, who alone was qualified to interpret certain prophecies.

- Typology rests on the belief that God's ways of acting are consistent throughout history.

- A promise-fulfillment scheme examines how the Old Testament anticipates and points towards climactic realization in the New Testament.

- Author-centered textual meaning is the position that a text means what the author intended and what its intended readers probably understood. This is the goal of biblical interpretation.

- Metaphorical discourse, such as parables, may be deliberately open-ended or polyvalent.

- Four criteria for establishing if an interpretation is probable: it is possible according to the norms of the language in which it was written; it accounts for each linguistic component in the text; it follows the conventions for its type of literature; and it must be coherent

• Four criteria for testing the potential validity of an interpretation: it conforms to orthodox Christian theology; it corresponds to typical paradigms of God's truth or activity; it works in the crucible of Christian experience; and it finds confirmation along the full spectrum of the orthodox faith-community

Reflection Questions

1. How would you answer the question of whether a modern reader can discover "new meaning" in a biblical text? Why? Can a text have multiple meanings? Why or why not? (p. 250)

2. Why do faithful Christian interpreters of Scripture come down on opposing sides of an issue like baptism? Why would God allow this kind of ambiguity in the Bible? What do these tensions teach us about biblical interpretation?

3. What are some of the difficulties in identifying one's own biases of interpretation? What might be some of your own biases? What biases have you observed in others?

Discussion Question

1. Do you believe that we can ever perceive a text's meaning or an author's intention with absolute accuracy? What are the challenges? What is the best we can do, in your opinion?

Quiz

1. _____ interpreters emphasize that a text may have many possible meanings.

a) Postmodern
b) Scholastic
c) Neo-orthodox
d) Reformed

2. The *sensus plenior* refers to the _____ of a text.

a) Plain, literal sense
b) Aesthetic beauty
c) Fuller sense
d) Literary framework

3. What was the hermeneutical key for early Christians in their interpretation and application of the Old Testament?

a) The coming of the Holy Spirit at Pentecost
b) The life, death, and resurrection of Jesus
c) The accounts of Jesus's miracles
d) Jesus's great commission to his disciples

4. Interpreters should strive to arrive at a text's _____ meaning.

a) Ordinary
b) Hidden
c) Doctrinal
d) Eschatological

5. (T/F) There appear to be instances where New Testament authors attribute meaning to or use an Old Testament text in ways that the Old Testament author did not intend.

6. (T/F) Biblical authors most likely intended their messages to have many meanings.

7. (T/F) A reader-oriented approach to interpretation focuses on discovering how the original readers would have read and understood a text.

8. (T/F) Literary approaches to studying the Bible are complementary to and equally important as historical concerns centered in the world of the author and text.

9. (T/F) Literary approaches to the Bible ought to allow interpreters to circumvent any concern for whether the biblical documents report genuine history.

10. (T/F) Fresh interpretations of Scripture must always and only be limited to the author's original perlocution.

CHAPTER 7

General Rules of Hermeneutics: Prose

You Should Know

- Literary context is the larger whole within which a specific text or passage is located.

- A pretext is an alleged interpretation that only appears to be valid, but in reality, obscures the real state of affairs.

- Contextualization requires us to look back into the biblical world to learn the intended meaning of a text and then to look at our own circumstances to determine how to express the meaning for today's world.

- Syncretism is the blending of religious beliefs to form a hybrid.

- A word is a semantic sign that marks out a field of meaning at a given time.

- The semantic field is the range of possible meanings for a particular word.

- A lexicon is a dictionary of ancient words, often including many examples of the use of each word, which helps students determine the range of meaning for a word.

- A concordance is a word study resource that provides students with all instances of a word's usage in the Bible.

- Syntax is the system within a language for combining its various linguistic constituents in order to communicate.

- Discourse analysis is the study of longer units of text, such as paragraphs or entire passages rather than individual clauses or sentences, in order to gain interpretive understanding.

Reflection Questions

1. What is proof-texting? Where have you seen it practiced? What are the dangers?

2. What does it mean that words have a field or range of meaning? How does this complicate interpretation and translation? What is an example of a word that is used several ways in Scripture?

3. Certain nuances of the biblical languages are lost in translation. What impact does this have on the transmission of the Word of God? Does this loss obscure any of the inspired and authoritative nature of Scripture? Why or why not?

Discussion Question

1. What is your standard practice for studying or interpreting Scripture? What practices of word, grammatical, and structural analysis that you read do you hope to incorporate into your biblical study in the future? Why?

Quiz

1. The largest literary context in which a biblical passage must be understood is:
    a) The whole biblical book in which it is found
    b) All the collected work of that biblical author
    c) The preceding and following paragraphs
    d) The entire canon of Scripture

2. The meaning of a specific text is most significantly controlled by its:
    a) Immediate context
    b) Book context

c) Testament context

d) Context of the entire Bible

3. Accurate interpretation requires that we understand a word in the same way:

a) The writer used it

b) The church has understood it

c) Textual scholars understand it

d) The Holy Spirit reveals it

4. The _____ meaning of a word refers to its direct sense or meaning.

a) Connotative

b) Denotative

c) Annotative

d) Referential

5. (T/F) Occurrences of a key word that are closer to the passage under study have greater weight for interpretation than occurrences of that word that are further away.

6. (T/F) Compiling the lexical meanings of the words of a passage gives the interpreter full understanding of that passage.

7. (T/F) Direct translations of one word after another yield the best English translations of the Bible.

8. (T/F) People who do not know Hebrew or Greek are at a disadvantage in the task of interpretation.

9. (T/F) All believers are competent to study the Bible.

10. (T/F) Bible interpreters should never refer to paraphrases of the Bible, such as Eugene Peterson's *The Message*.

ANSWER KEY

1. D, 2. A, 3. A, 4. B, 5. T, 6. F, 7. F, 8. T, 9. T, 10. F

CHAPTER 8

General Rules of Hermeneutics: Biblical Poetry

You Should Know

- The form of Hebrew poetry is free rhythm, which is characterized neither by lock-step meter nor by unanchored free verse.

- Assonance is a poetic sound device where the author repeats certain vowel sounds.

- Alliteration is a poetic sound device where the author repeats certain consonant sounds.

- Paronomasia or wordplay is a poetic device where two similar-sounding words are contrasted or juxtaposed.

- Parallelism is a defining feature of Hebrew poetry, whereby two or more successive poetic lines dynamically strengthen, reinforce, and develop each other's thought.

- The three traditional kinds of Hebrew parallelism: synonymous; antithetical; and synthetic

- Chiasm is a structural device in which the word order of a parallel line is the reverse of its predecessor (*a b, b' a'*).

- *Merismus* is a literary device where a writer mentions the extremes of some category in order to portray it as a totality (p. 394); (example: "From the least of them to the greatest" Jer 31:34)

- *Inclusio* is a structural device in which a unit of text is framed by repeating words or phrases from its opening lines again at its conclusion.

- Eisegesis means reading a meaning into a text that the text itself does not intend.

Reflection Questions

1. Why do you think God chose to communicate his Word via poetry rather than simply via propositional facts and information? If you had to teach about biblical poetry in your context, what would be your main points?

2. What is an *inclusio*? What does an *inclusio* highlight about the passage? Can you think of one or two examples?

3. The prophets use vivid imagery to indict God's people (and her neighbors). What can contemporary preachers learn from these prophets? How would you react if you heard a preacher speaking like one of the Hebrew prophets?

Discussion Question

1. What do you appreciate about the poetry and poetic language in the Bible? What do you struggle with? Do you tend to lean more towards the poetic sections in your reading, or do you avoid them? Why?

Quiz

1. Approximately how much of the Bible does poetry comprise?
   a) One-quarter
   b) One-third
   c) One-half
   d) Two-thirds

2. Poetry tends to use concrete images to convey:
   a) A concrete idea
   b) An abstract idea

    c) Reason

    d) Facts

3. Poetry appeals most to:
   - a) Reason
   - b) Emotion
   - c) Imagination
   - d) Creativity

4. "Where, O death, is your victory?" is an example of:
   - a) Hyperbole
   - b) Apostrophe
   - c) Metonymy
   - d) Synecdoche

5. The book of Song of Songs is composed as a(n):
   - a) Acrostic
   - b) Chiasm
   - c) *Merismus*
   - d) Synecdoche

6. "From the least of them to the greatest" is an example of:
   - a) Chiasm
   - b) *Inclusio*
   - c) Alliteration
   - d) *Merismus*

7. (T/F) Biblical Hebrew poets nearly always used the same sound devices as English poets do, i.e., rhyme and meter.

8. (T/F) Hebrew poetry operates within certain poetic limitations and patterns.

9. (T/F) None of the metric poetic features of Hebrew poetry are discernible in English translations.

10. (T/F) Biblical Greek, unlike Hebrew, never uses assonance or alliteration.

ANSWER KEY

1. B, 2. B, 3. C, 4. B, 5. B, 6. D, 7. F, 8. T, 9. F, 10. F

CHAPTER 9

Genres of the Old Testament

You Should Know

- An anecdote is a report that details an event or experience in the life of a person, in other words, more private biography than public history.

- A memoir is a report written in the first person about incidents in the life of an individual.

- A heroic narrative is a series of episodes that focus on the life and exploits of a hero whom people later consider significant enough to remember.

- An epic is a type of heroic narrative, usually lengthy and episodic, in which the exploits of the hero are magnified to a scale of great importance for the nation, usually displaying strong nationalistic interest.

- A comedy is a narrative whose plot has a happy ending, in some cases through a dramatic reversal. Old Testament examples include Esther and Joseph.

- The *lex talionis* or law of retaliation is the law that the punishment must match the crime in nature and proportion: eye for eye, tooth for tooth, hand for hand, etc. (Exodus 21:23–25).

- A suzerain-vassal treaty, used by the Hittites and Assyrians, dictated the relationship between a major power and its subject nations. The structure of Deuteronomy closely resembles this form of treaty.

- Elements of a suzerain-vassal treaty: a historical prologue; a list of stipulations; mention of witnesses; and blessings and curses

- The most common genre among the prophets is the prophecy of disaster, an announcement of imminent or future devastation either to an individual or to an entire nation.

- In apocalyptic prophecy God reveals his hidden future plans, usually through dreams or visions with elaborate and strange symbolism or numbers.

Reflection Questions

1. What does it mean when Genesis 1–11 is described as a cosmic epic? What are the epic elements? How does understanding these chapters as an epic help you to interpret them?

2. You read that "readers must interpret the law relationally." What does this mean? What impact does this have on your interpretation of Old Testament law? How would you explain what it means that Jesus "fulfilled" the law? How does this clarify your approach to interpreting the laws in the Old Testament?

3. What challenges do Christians face in interpreting prophetic literature? Why is it difficult for Christians to know how to handle the prophets?

Discussion Question

1. Where have you encountered someone misusing or misreading a text of Scripture because of not taking into account the text's genre? Describe the passage and explain the misuse. What was the impact on their interpretation?

Quiz

1. At one-third of the whole, _____ is the most common literature form in the Old Testament.

- a) Narrative
- b) Poetry
- c) Law
- d) Prophecy

2. A series of reports compiled together and consciously structured to underscore connections between events and to sound certain themes is called a(n):

- a) History
- b) Anecdote
- c) Memoir
- d) Speech

3. The book of Esther can be classified as a(n):

- a) Prophet story
- b) Epic
- c) Comedy
- d) Tragedy

4. The book of _____ offers a comprehensive restatement of the Mosaic Law.

- a) Leviticus
- b) Joshua
- c) 1 Chronicles
- d) Deuteronomy

5. The book of Habakkuk is an example of a:

- a) Dialogue of protest
- b) Prophetic disputation
- c) Prophecy of salvation
- d) Prophetic narrative

6. The primary genre of wisdom literature in the book of Job is:

- a) Instruction
- b) Disputation
- c) Example story
- d) Reflection

7. (T/F) Prophetic books usually exhibit clear order and development of material and themes.

8. (T/F) The protest constitutes the most common genre of prayer in the psalms.

9. (T/F) In most cases, Old Testament prophecies about Israel and Zion find their fulfillment spiritually in the church.

10. (T/F) Proverbs teach absolute, unbending truth.

CHAPTER 10

Genres of the New Testament

You Should Know

- Gospel (Greek *euangelion*) means "good news."

- Q: proposed collection of Jesus's sayings common to both Matthew and Luke but not found in Mark

- The Jesus Seminar: group of critical scholars who color-coded the sayings and narratives of Jesus found in the four canonical Gospels and the Gospel of Thomas based on their apparent authenticity

- Redaction criticism attempts to discover the historical and theological perspectives of a biblical writer by analyzing the editorial and compositional techniques and interpretations used to shape the text.

- Inaugurated eschatology is the view that the kingdom of God arrived in part at Christ's first coming but awaits its full consummation at his return.

- Many scholars view several of the New Testament Epistles as pseudonymous, meaning they were written in the name of a leading Christian figure by someone else, perhaps a generation or more later.

- Three major types of Greco-Roman rhetoric include judicial—seeking to convince an audience of the rightness or wrongness of a past action; deliberative—trying to persuade or dissuade an audience regarding a future action; and epideictic—using praise or blame to urge an audience to affirm a point of view or set of values.

- Covenantal nomism refers to the idea from the "new perspective on Paul" that, for Jews, obedience to the Law identified one as a member of the exclusive covenant community God established with Israel.

Reflection Questions

1. What does it mean to say that thinking vertically should take priority over thinking horizontally when considering the Gospels? Why is this important?

2. What does it mean to say that conservative evangelical *applications* of Gospel miracles (what they have to do with "my life") have differed very little from more liberal demythologizing? Why do you think this is the case?

3. How do you assess the debate over the core of Paul's theology sparked by the New Perspective on Paul? Which position do you side with strongest? Why?

Discussion Question

1. Name two differences between two or more reports of the same story in the Gospels. Do you find any of the differences to be troubling? Why or why not? How would you respond to someone who argued that these differences undermine the reliability of the Gospels?

Quiz

1. _____ shows a particular interest in showing Jesus as the friend of sinners and outcasts in Jewish society.
   a) Matthew
   b) Mark
   c) Luke
   d) John

2. _____ was likely written to reassure and encourage a Gentile-Christian audience as imperial persecution against Christians intensified.

a) Matthew
b) Mark
c) Luke
d) John

3. Inaugurated _____ refers to the "already but not yet" nature of the kingdom of God.
a) Eschatology
b) Soteriology
c) Pneumatology
d) Axiology

4. The book of Acts bears a strong resemblance to the _____ genre.
a) Prophetic
b) Gospel
c) Apocalyptic
d) Wisdom

5. Revelation combines parts of these three distinct genres:
a) Epistle, prophecy, and apocalyptic
b) Epistle, wisdom, and Gospel
c) Wisdom, prophecy, and apocalyptic
d) Prophecy, apocalyptic, and cosmic epic

6. (T/F) The best application of miracle stories is to distill them down to a moral principle or injunction for all times and places.

7. (T/F) Since narrative literature in the Bible often teaches less directly than didactic literature, it should therefore be taken as less normative.

8. (T/F) The New Testament authors wrote their epistles for specific occasions to address particular audiences facing unique problems.

9. (T/F) New Testament epistles show strong parallels to conventional Greco-Roman letters.

10. (T/F) The epistle of James appears to be a collection of teachings loosely strung together, like the book of Proverbs.

CHAPTER 11

Using the Bible Today

You Should Know

- Worship is the activity that occurs when people respond to God's revelation of himself and how he has acted in Jesus Christ.

- "But you are a chosen people, a royal priesthood, a holy nation, God's special possession, that you may declare the praises of him who called you out of darkness into his wonderful light. Once you were not a people, but now you are the people of God; once you had not received mercy, but now you have received mercy" (1 Peter 2:9–10).

- The worldviews or belief systems of theists can be termed "theologies."

- Biblical theology is that discipline which sets forth the message of the books of the Bible in their historical setting.

- Systematic theology strives to give a coherent statement of the doctrines of Christianity for contemporary readers.

- Guidelines for formulating theology on the basis of the Bible: follow the conclusions of sound exegesis on appropriate texts; look at the Bible's total teaching on an issue; determine the Bible's own emphases about an issue; state the significance for the church; center theology in what God has revealed; and compare conclusions with others

- "All Scripture is God-breathed and is useful for teaching, rebuking, correcting and training in righteousness" (2 Timothy 3:16).

- The Reformation rallying cry *sola scriptura* highlights that theology must be centered in Scripture.

- The ultimate question of our interpretive work is whether we will submit to God's instructions and expectations.

Reflection Questions

1. Christians begin with the presupposition that God conveys reliable information in Scripture. Where does this leave unbelievers who approach the text? What is their access point to possible faith if they don't begin with this presupposition?

2. You read that theological affirmations must reflect the Bible's total teaching, not some isolated texts. How does this temper the tendency of those who proof-text all their claims? How can you strive to represent more carefully the Bible's total teaching in your theological affirmations on a topic?

3. What are the differences between preaching and teaching? How would you describe the central goal of each task? Do you think one is more important than the other? Why?

Discussion Question

1. Explain the differences between biblical and systematic theology. What are the advantages to, and limitations of, each? Which are you more interested in studying? Why?

Quiz

1. _____ revelation refers to the Bible, which reveals truth not available from any other source.

    a) General
    b) Exclusive
    c) Special
    d) Orthodox

2. _____ studies the development of theology within the historical movement of the Bible itself.

a) Historical theology
b) Biblical theology
c) Systematic theology
d) Developmental theology

3. The Reformation principle of _____ led to a denigration within Protestantism of the church's rich heritage and tradition.

a) *Sola scriptura*
b) *Ad fontes*
c) *Sola gratia*
d) *Sola fide*

4. The practice of preaching probably began:

a) In the early church
b) During the Reformation
c) With Jesus
d) In the post-exilic period

5. _____ preaching sticks close to the actual structure of the biblical text.

a) Narrative
b) Expository
c) Anagogic
d) New Testament

6. _____ Christians are those who are Christian in name only.

a) Nominal
b) Prescriptive
c) Orthodox
d) Cognitive

7. (T/F) The categories of systematic theology are those of the theologian's making, not necessarily those of the biblical writer.

8. (T/F) The approaches of biblical theology, as opposed to systematic theology, tend to expose and highlight the inherent diversity of the Bible.

9. (T/F) Valid theology must be practical and should be stated in

ways that explain and illuminate the significance of its teachings for the life and ministry of the church today.

10. (T/F) Personal spiritual formation ought to remain a private inner issue.

CHAPTER 12

Application

You Should Know

- Meaning vs. significance is a distinction between the ideas a text originally intended to communicate and the implications of that intention for later readers.

- Principlizing refers to the attempt to discover a text's spiritual, moral, or theological principles that have relevance for today (p. 610).

- Sequence of the four-step methodology for legitimate application: determine the original application(s); apply transferable applications appropriately; if not transferable, identify cross-cultural principles of the text; and find appropriate applications of those principles

- Creation ordinance refers to a principle for how people should live that God established prior to the fall of humanity into sin.

- A redemptive movement hermeneutic suggests that the trajectory of biblical thought may mean Christians today should move beyond the New Testament in their application.

- A purpose/intent statement occurs when Scripture gives a reason for a command, which may require a different application in a different culture to preserve the command's intent.

- The presence of levels of authority indicates that the closer the modern application corresponds to the application in the biblical text, the greater the degree of confidence we can have that our application is legitimate.

- Five crucial elements for proper interpretation and application:

spiritual rebirth; spiritual maturity; diligent study; common sense and logic; and humble dependence on the Spirit

Reflection Questions

1. How would you describe meaning vs. significance, and the importance of this distinction, to people in your church community?

2. How would you describe "principlizing" to someone in your church? Why might this be a helpful tool for thinking about application of biblical texts?

3. How can you figure out how an Old Testament text has been fulfilled in Christ? What principles guide the interpretive process?

Discussion Question

1. What instances have you encountered or heard about where people from different cultures applied biblical teaching on a topic in starkly different ways? How can you account for the differences? Was one interpretation better than the other? Why or why not?

Quiz

1. The Old Testament forbids putting tattoo marks on a person because:
   a) Tattoos mar the image of God
   b) Tattoos were associated with pagan worship
   c) The people did not have sanitary means of administering tattoos
   d) Only the high priest was permitted to have a single tattoo

2. In the process of tempting Jesus, the devil:
   a) Denied the claims of Scripture
   b) Misquoted parts of Scripture

   c) Did not mention Scripture

   d) Correctly quoted but poorly applied Scripture

3. Early Christians practiced marketplace evangelism primarily because:

   a) Public arenas were the socially acceptable places to consider new ideas

   b) The market was where they could reach the biggest crowds

   c) They were forbidden from entering the synagogues

   d) It was expected that they would provide meals for their listeners

4. In its ancient Near Eastern cultural background, the "eye for an eye, tooth for a tooth" law:

   a) Was a vindictive call for revenge

   b) Provided a way to publicly shame the offender

   c) Was radically limiting in preventing excessive punishment

   d) Was universal and therefore assumed by everyone in that context

5. The most important condition for God to answer prayer is:

   a) That the believer pray repeatedly

   b) That the request be in accordance with God's will

   c) That the request be for the mutual good of the community

   d) That the request has an evangelistic purpose

6. Interpretation of Scripture falls short of its intended goal if interpreters do not:

   a) Pray and rely on the Holy Spirit for guidance

   b) Memorize Scripture

   c) Teach others what they learn

   d) Verify their interpretation against the Christian creeds

7. (T/F) To interpret the New Testament consistently, we must apply our understanding of the teaching on homosexual practices in the same way we apply our understanding of teachings on slavery and women.

8. (T/F) If we follow closely all the steps of good interpretation, we will be equally certain of all our applications of various biblical texts.

9. (T/F) Faithful application of Scripture requires only that we earnestly study Scripture itself.

10. (T/F) The Holy Spirit does not give new interpretation on par with Scripture.

www.ingramcontent.com/pod-product-compliance
Lightning Source LLC
Chambersburg PA
CBHW010038040426
42331CB00037B/3303